RAISING A TEEN, BECOMING A PARENT

A Compassionate Guide for Parents in a Changing World

By Venkata Krishna Rao Machineni

Preface

Parenting a teenager is like holding the hand of someone walking into a storm—and sometimes, pulling away from you while doing it. This book was born out of real conversations—some tender, some tearful—with parents, educators, teens, and grandparents. A pattern became clear: teenage years aren't just turbulent for the child. They're transformative for the parent.

As an educator and parent rooted in Indian life but engaged globally, I've seen teens crave the same things across countries—understanding, connection, and belief in their potential. But they are growing up in a faster, noisier world than we ever knew. And they need us more than they admit.

This book is not a manual. It is a mirror. It blends timeless wisdom with modern insights, Indian experiences

with global relevance. It invites you to
walk beside your teen—not ahead to
drag, nor behind to chase, but beside,
with presence and patience.

May these pages hold light for the
paths you and your child will walk—
together.

— Venkata Krishna Rao Machineni

Table of Contents

Chapter 1: Inside the Teenage Brain

"What lies behind us and what lies before us are tiny matters compared to what lies within us." — Ralph Waldo Emerson

In the quiet, copper-toned rooftops of Warangal, thirteen-year-old Anay sat in silence. The sun was melting behind the temple tower, but he didn't notice. He was gripped by something invisible yet powerful—a feeling that churned his chest, made his palms cold, and filled his throat with unsaid things. He had just had an argument with his best friend—over something small, petty even. But the pain wasn't small. His mother, noticing his restlessness, sat beside him. She didn't offer advice. She didn't correct. She simply offered a cup of tea and said, 'I used to cry like that, too.'

That moment would later mark a turning point. Not because the problem was solved. But because Anay felt seen.

Adolescence isn't a phase where a child becomes difficult—it's a phase where they begin becoming someone new. Their brain is literally under construction. The amygdala, the emotional center, is operating at full strength. Meanwhile, the prefrontal cortex—the part that helps with reasoning and impulse control—is still developing.

This explains a teenager's paradox: why they might ace an exam but forget to eat lunch; why they cry over a lost phone charger but dismiss serious conversations. It's not irrationality. It's biology.

A 2021 global neuroscience study published in Nature Reviews Neuroscience confirmed that adolescent brain development is marked by a surge in emotional

reactivity and a temporary dip in
self-regulation. In India, a survey by
YourDOST Mental Health Platform
revealed that over 39% of teens
reported frequent emotional
overwhelm, often misunderstood by
parents as 'attitude.'

Ancient epics, from the Mahabharata
to the Iliad, are filled with teenage
heroes—bold, emotional, and
conflicted. Abhimanyu and Achilles
both faced battles they only half-
understood. Incomplete knowledge,
untested courage—they are not
flaws. They are features of youth.

But today's battlefield is different.
It's on screens. In Snapchat streaks,
Instagram likes, and WhatsApp
silence.

The digital brain grows up
differently. Dopamine spikes from
notifications, the illusion of
connection, and the curated lives of
peers online create constant
emotional noise. A teen may not

remember what they studied, but they will remember how many likes they got—or didn't get—that day.

Across continents, silence is often misread. In many Asian and Indian households, a quiet teen is praised for being 'obedient.' In Western homes, that same silence may cause alarm. But across cultures, silence often signals the same thing: emotional saturation.

In a café in Paris, a father once said of his daughter, 'She's become distant.' In a classroom in Tokyo, a teacher whispered, 'He's tired, but he won't say.' And in Hyderabad, a mother said, 'He's not himself anymore.'

The language changes. The feeling does not.

Anay, at 17, now in college, walks into the campus library when it rains. Not because he needs a book. But because the rain reminds him of sitting on that rooftop, of his mother's quiet presence. The memory brings him calm.

Meanwhile, halfway across the world, in São Paulo, Luiza—also 17—listens to the rain against her dorm window. She remembers her father's voice telling her that emotions are not interruptions—they are data.

Both teens, shaped by different cultures, found peace in the same thing: being seen. Not analyzed. Not corrected. But understood.

As a parent, you are not here to 'fix' your teen. You are here to guide them while they fix themselves. Like a gardener, you don't control the fruit. You tend the roots.

What they need is your steadiness, not your solutions. Your willingness to listen, not your lecture. Your faith in them, especially when they don't have it for themselves.

And sometimes, all they need is to
hear you say:

'This feeling you have? It's not a
flaw. It's a sign that you're growing.'

Because the teenage brain isn't a war
zone. It's a growing forest. And all
forests are wild before they are
beautiful.

Brain Region	Function	Effect on Teen Behavior
Amygdala	Processes emotions like fear, anger, joy	Heightened emotional reactivity
Prefrontal Cortex	Controls planning, impulse, judgment	Underdeveloped – impulsive behavior
Nucleus Accumbens	Handles reward, motivation	Drawn to stimulation (social media, risks)
Neuroplasticity	Brain rewiring capacity	Highly influenced by environment & support

Chapter 2: Communication That Builds Trust

"Speak only if it improves upon the silence." — Mahatma Gandhi

In the dimly lit living room of a Bengaluru apartment, 15-year-old Ravi sat cross-legged on the sofa, scrolling through his phone. Earbuds in. Hoodie up. His father, Rajesh, paused at the doorway, wanting to say something, anything—but unsure where to start. He turned to his wife and said, almost in a whisper, "He never talks anymore."

What Rajesh didn't know is that Ravi had sent twelve messages that day—just not to his family. Teenagers don't stop communicating. They just change their language.

Today's adolescents communicate in memes, emojis, silence, and sarcasm. Their emotional grammar is encoded in eye rolls, song lyrics, Instagram stories, and passive-aggressive "seen" receipts. According to a 2022 UNICEF study, over 74% of teenagers worldwide feel safer expressing difficult emotions digitally than face-to-face.

In Indian households, communication often defaults to interrogation. "Did you study?" "Why are you wasting time?" These aren't conversations. They're checklists.

Teenagers, especially in India, crave curiosity—not control. They want to be asked, "What made you smile today?" or "What's something that annoyed you?" They don't want immediate advice. They want acknowledgment.

Meenakshi, a schoolteacher in Coimbatore, introduced a ritual with her teenage son: every night, she asked, "What's one thing you didn't say today?" Some nights, he said nothing. Some nights, he opened up.

In Stockholm, 16-year-old Elin wrote in her journal, "My mom asks how I'm doing but waits for the answer she wants, not the one I have." Her mother eventually changed tactics. She stopped asking and started sharing—her awkward teenage years, heartbreaks, and moments of self-doubt. And slowly, Elin began to talk.

In the Ramayana, Hanuman rediscovers his strength not through pressure but presence. When Jambavan reminds him of his power, Hanuman rises—not just physically but emotionally. Teens don't need loud reminders. They need silent witnesses to their becoming.

Instead of "Why are you always on your phone?" try "Show me something you laughed at today." Instead of "What's wrong with you?" try "You seem off—want to talk or just sit together?"

Psychologists refer to the "shutdown reflex"—when teens expect judgment, they preemptively go silent. To break this cycle, parents must offer something radical: safe silence.

One rainy evening, Rajesh left a sticky note on Ravi's study table: "No questions. No advice. Just this—I see you. And I love you." The next morning, he found Ravi in the kitchen, quiet but present. That was the first conversation in weeks. It wasn't long. But it was real.

Your teen won't remember every word you say. But they will remember the night you sat beside them without needing to fix them. The joke you cracked during their meltdown. The silent tea you shared when words weren't ready.

Communication is not about saying more. It's about meaning more. It's not about the cleverness of your words—but the softness of your presence.

Use the following checklist to reflect on your communication style:

Common Phrase	A Better Alternative
Did you finish your homework?	What was interesting in what you studied today?
Stop wasting time!	What do you feel like doing right now—and why?
You never talk to us.	Is there something you wish I'd ask—without judgment?
What's wrong with you?	You seem low. Want to talk or just hang out quietly?

Chapter 3: Boundaries Without Battles

"Discipline is the bridge between goals and accomplishment." — Jim Rohn

On the edge of a sugarcane field in Belagavi, 14-year-old Raghav watched his father fix a fence—not to trap anyone in, but to keep wild cattle out. He asked, "Why don't we just let it all grow wild?" His father smiled, "Because freedom without form is chaos."

Years later, when Raghav became a father, that phrase returned to him every time his teenage daughter slammed her door or broke a curfew. Parenting a teen feels like a tug-of-war between trust and control. But what if the goal isn't to win—but to let go just enough?

Teenagers don't hate rules. They hate rules that feel unfair, unexplained, or controlling. A 2021 Harvard study showed teens are 43% more likely to follow rules they help create.

In many Indian homes, however, rules arrive like commandments— "Because I said so." The result? Not obedience, but quiet rebellion. Silence. Secrets. And the erosion of trust.

Take Neha, a 15-year-old in Chennai. Her parents believed in structure—dinner at 8, lights out by 10, phones off by 9. It worked. Until it didn't. When Neha turned 15, she started lying about study hours, sneaking her phone into bed, and staying up late with friends.

But things shifted when her father said, "Let's make a new plan— together." They renegotiated curfews, phone time, and expectations. The result wasn't just fewer arguments. It was a stronger bond.

Indian mythology often celebrates obedience—Eklavya offering his thumb, Rama accepting exile. But today's teens aren't living epics. They are navigating complexity, technology, identity, and peer pressure. They don't need blind rules. They need evolving frameworks.

Sophia, a mother in Vancouver, allowed her daughter to take one day off school per month—no questions asked. "Mental health days," she called them. At first, her daughter abused the freedom. But in time, she respected it. Eventually, she barely used it.

Boundaries are not about power. They are about safety. Teens test them to know we care. But when those boundaries are explained and flexible, they become trusted rails—not walls.

Raghav, now grown, walks every Sunday with his teenage daughter.

Sometimes she talks. Sometimes she doesn't. But she knows he listens. Last week she said, "Appa, I think I messed up." He didn't yell. He didn't correct. He just said, "Tell me everything."

That night, she redefined her own boundary—not because she had to, but because she wanted to.

The following table shows how a typical parent-teen power struggle can be transformed into a collaborative boundary-setting moment:

Traditional Reaction	Collaborative Alternative
"You're grounded!"	"How do you think we can rebuild trust?"
"No phones after 9 PM because I said so."	"Let's agree on a screen curfew that works for both of us."
"You broke the rule again!"	"What made it hard to follow the rule? Let's talk."
"You're not going out this weekend."	"If we revisit this rule together, what would you change?"

Chapter 4: Mental Health Matters

"Feelings are much like waves; we can't stop them from coming, but we can choose which ones to surf." — Jonatan Mårtensson

One morning in Kochi, 16-year-old Tara stayed in bed long after her alarm rang. Her books were untouched. Her phone buzzed with messages from classmates. Her mother knocked once, then twice, then slowly entered the room. Tara looked up, her eyes red. 'I don't know why I'm like this,' she whispered.

In that sentence was a whole world of emotion neither of them could explain—at least not quickly. Tara wasn't lazy. She wasn't disobedient. She was exhausted. Quietly drowning in expectations, comparison, and the invisible burden of trying to hold everything together.

Across India—and the world—
teenagers are enduring a silent storm
of mental fatigue. According to a
2022 report by the Indian Psychiatry
Society, one in seven Indian teens is
likely to suffer from depression or
anxiety, often without a diagnosis.
The World Health Organization
reported a 35% rise in adolescent
emotional distress globally in the last
decade.

What's changed? The pressure to
perform, to fit in, to 'be someone'—
all amplified by the never-ending
scroll of social media. In Pune, 17-
year-old Isha checked WhatsApp at
2 AM just to confirm she hadn't
been removed from a group chat.
Her self-worth began to hinge on
notifications.

She started skipping dinner. Stopped
smiling. When asked if she was
okay, her answer was always the
same: 'I'm fine.' Until one day, she
wasn't. Her father, a school librarian,

found a crumpled diary page in the dustbin. It read, 'I wish someone would notice I'm not okay—before I have to explain it.'

Teens rarely say, 'I'm depressed.' They say:
- I'm tired.
- Leave me alone.
- Nothing matters.

Or worse—they say nothing at all.

In Indian homes, emotional health is still often interpreted as weakness. Responses like "We didn't have these problems in our time" or "This is nothing. Toughen up" are common. But today's teenagers are living in a more complex, louder, and less forgiving world. Resilience matters—but empathy must walk beside it.

You don't have to be a therapist to support your teen. But you can be their safe space. You can:
- Normalize emotional expression:

'It's okay to cry.'
- Share your own struggles: 'I've
been afraid too.'
- Respect their silence without
interpreting it as rebellion.
- Suggest counseling without shame
or fear.

Simple rituals—like evening walks,
playlists made together, or sitting
with them without expectations—act
as emotional anchors. Tara's mother
didn't tell her to cheer up. She folded
the blanket beside her and said, 'You
don't need to explain anything. Just
breathe.' That night, they baked
cookies together—half-burnt but
healing.

Your teen doesn't need you to
understand everything. They need
you to stay. To be their steady
presence in a world that feels
unpredictable and loud. To be their
first safe home.

Use the table below to help
distinguish between ordinary mood

changes and signs that your child may need mental health support:

Behavior	May Indicate...	Suggested Parental Response
Sleeping all day	Possible depression or withdrawal	Gently ask, 'Would it help to talk or do something together?'
Irritability or snapping	Internal stress or overwhelm	Offer space followed by calm curiosity
Loss of interest in things they enjoyed	Anhedonia (early sign of depression)	Share a memory and invite, not force, engagement
Saying 'I'm tired' constantly	Emotional fatigue or anxiety	Normalize rest and open the door to conversation

Chapter 5: Digital Lives, Real Emotions

"Technology is a useful servant but a dangerous master." — Christian Lous Lange

In a dusty village near Guntur, 15-year-old Meera hid under a neem tree, phone in hand. She wasn't texting friends. She was watching a YouTube video on physics. It was the only coaching she had access to. But when her mother saw her screen, the reaction was immediate: "Always on the phone! Study first!"

Meanwhile, in Mumbai, 16-year-old Aditya spent five hours daily flipping between Instagram reels and Discord chats. He laughed. He shared. But by night, he felt oddly empty—as if all that noise hadn't touched him at all.

Today's teens live double lives—one in the physical world, the other on a screen. They celebrate birthdays in person and on Snapchat. They argue in school and apologize via emoji. Their emotional ecosystems are deeply entangled with technology.

A 2023 ICMR report showed that Indian teens spend an average of 3.5 to 5 hours per day on screens. More concerning, 52% said they feel anxious or inadequate after scrolling social media. Digital validation—likes, comments, hearts—can feel more real than face-to-face praise.

But banning phones won't solve the problem. That creates secrecy, not safety. Instead, we need to engage with their digital lives as we do with their school life: curiously, non-judgmentally, and collaboratively.

In one Hyderabad household, parents hosted a 'tech night'—once a week, everyone shared a favorite app, game, or video. It created understanding and reduced judgment. The phone stopped being a wedge. It became a window.

Teens often hear, "You're addicted to your phone." But they rarely hear, "Is something online making you anxious?" We must move from accusation to inquiry.

As parents, we need to model what balance looks like. A parent who is always on WhatsApp cannot expect digital restraint from their teen. Set boundaries together—not as rulers, but as cohabitants of the same digital planet.

Technology isn't going away. And neither is your teen's connection to it. But connection doesn't have to mean control. It can mean shared discovery, healthy limits, and open eyes.

The real goal is not to disconnect them from devices—but to reconnect them with themselves.

Use the following table as a guide to create a healthier screen relationship in your family:

Concern	Instead of Saying...	Try This Instead
Excessive screen time	"You're always on that phone!"	"Let's agree on tech-free hours together."
Anxiety after social media	"Why do you care what others post?"	"Does anything online ever make you feel small?"
Late-night usage	"No phones after 10, period."	"How do you feel in the morning after late scrolling?"
Gaming conflict	"This game is ruining your life!"	"Can we schedule play time and breaks together?"

Chapter 6: Peer Pressure & Identity Search

"Be yourself; everyone else is already taken." — Oscar Wilde

In a schoolyard in Ahmedabad, 14-year-old Kiran refused to smoke a cigarette his friends offered him. But when they laughed and called him a baby, he hesitated. He didn't want the smoke. But he also didn't want to be left out.

In Toronto, 16-year-old Naomi started wearing oversized jackets and hiding her poetry journal. Her friends were all into sports, and she didn't want to seem 'too sensitive'. She once told her mom, "It's easier to fit in than to stand out."

Teenagers aren't just discovering what they like—they're discovering who they are. And often, identity is shaped in contrast to those around them. They want to belong. But belonging can come with a cost.

Peer pressure is not always loud. Sometimes, it's a silence when everyone laughs at the same joke. Sometimes, it's the way a teen changes their phone wallpaper because a friend said it was childish. It's subtle, social, and relentless.

Adolescence is a time of identity formation. Erik Erikson, a developmental psychologist, described it as the stage of 'Identity vs. Role Confusion'. Teens ask: Who am I, apart from who my parents want me to be? Who am I when I'm not being watched?

In Indian households, this search is often layered with expectations—cultural norms, family values, academic aspirations. A boy who likes music may be nudged toward engineering. A girl who questions religion may be asked to stay quiet. But identity doesn't flourish under silence. It grows in curiosity and safe disagreement.

Romantic curiosity is also part of this journey. Many Indian parents panic when their teen develops feelings or friendships that seem too close. But shutting down the conversation doesn't end the exploration. It only moves it underground.

Instead of fearing the influence of peers, help your teen learn to evaluate it. Ask, "How did you feel after spending time with them?" instead of "Are they a good influence?" Trust is built not by control, but by connection.

As your teen tests boundaries and social waters, remind them that identity is not about performance— it's about presence. They don't have to be anyone else to be accepted at home.

And remind yourself: your job is not to prevent them from getting lost.

It's to be the landmark they can return to when they're ready to be found.

Here's a quick guide to help you understand when to step in, and when to step back:

Situation	Step In When...	Step Back When...
New friend group	Values conflict with your family's or safety is a concern	They're bonding over common interests or harmless fun
Romantic interest	There's secrecy, manipulation, or emotional distress	They're talking openly and showing responsibility
Change in dress/music/habits	It's causing harm or is clearly a cry for help	It's part of normal experimentation or expression
Requests for freedom	There's risk of danger or deceit	They're negotiating respectfully and keeping communication open

Chapter 7: Academic Pressure & Parental Expectations

"Expectation is the root of all heartache." — William Shakespeare

At a coaching center in Hyderabad, 17-year-old Aarav looked at the rank list and sighed. He wasn't at the top. Again. His parents hadn't scolded him, but their silence over dinner spoke louder than words.

In Indore, 16-year-old Riya got a 94% in her board exams. Her cousin had 96%. Her uncle joked, "Just 2% behind Sharma ji's daughter." Everyone laughed. Riya didn't.

Academic pressure in India is deeply cultural. It's not just about marks. It's about pride, marriage prospects, family honor, and future security. But when dreams are weighed down by obligation, ambition becomes anxiety.

According to a 2023 NIMHANS study, 52% of Indian high school students report academic stress as their top source of anxiety. JEE, NEET, CUET—these are not just exams. They are identity tests. And the pressure is often invisible.

Parents don't intend to hurt. They want the best. But phrases like "We're counting on you" or "You have to do what we couldn't" become emotional baggage. Encouragement, when not balanced with empathy, turns into pressure.

But what's the difference between pressure and support? Often, it's tone. It's timing. It's whether your teen feels seen as a person or judged as a performance.

In a society where marks often define merit, parents have a sacred role—not to add weight, but to carry it with compassion. Ask your teen, "What's one thing you wish I

understood about your studies?" and
really listen.

Aarav, after months of pressure,
eventually told his parents he wanted
to study physics—not for rank, but
for research. They listened. And
slowly, pressure became passion.

Not every child is a topper. But
every child has potential. And the
difference between the two is often
not intelligence—but the safety to
grow without fear.

Here's a table to help reflect on how pressure can be transformed into support:

Feels Like Pressure When...	Feels Like Support When...
You say 'You must crack this exam.'	You say 'We're proud of your effort, no matter the result.'
You compare them to others.	You compare them only to their past self.
You talk only about studies.	You ask about their well-being too.
Success is the only acceptable outcome.	Learning is celebrated, even when mistakes happen.

Chapter 8: Building Bonds That Last

"Children may not remember what you said, but they will always remember how you made them feel."
— Carl W. Buehner

In the foothills of Mussoorie, a father and daughter took a walk every Sunday—rain or shine. Sometimes they talked about school. Sometimes about nothing. One week, she ranted about exams. The next, she walked silently, headphones in. Still, he showed up. Every Sunday.

When she turned eighteen and moved to Delhi for college, he received a letter. It read: 'I don't remember everything you said. But I remember that you walked with me. And that saved me.'

Bonding with your teenager doesn't require big gestures. It demands presence. Emotional availability—

especially when they're least lovable. Teens don't always articulate their feelings, but they notice everything:

- That you kept your word
- That you respected their privacy
- That you didn't give up on them when they pushed you away

In a Telugu folktale, a boy asks his grandfather why he plants trees he may never sit under. The old man smiles: "Because one day, you will." That is parenting. Planting shade you may never use—but knowing it will matter.

In Finland, a mother named Leena left handwritten notes on her son's door every week. 'Good luck on your test.' 'I love your music.' 'You're stronger than you know.' He never responded. Never even acknowledged them. But when he left for college, he took them all.

Psychologist Dr. Dan Siegel calls this 'mindsight'—the ability to make someone feel felt. Teens don't need fixes. They need to feel seen beneath their silence. Recognized beyond their rebellion.

Dr. John Gottman's research shows that consistent 'emotional bids'—small moments of connection—have a deeper impact than long, structured 'quality time.' In other words, it's not the family vacation they'll remember. It's the messy dinner where everyone laughed.

Try these seven small ways to build connection without pressure:

1. Leave a Post-it note on their book with encouragement.

2. Ask 'Do you want advice or just company?'

3. Watch a movie they love—even if you don't get it.

4. Sit beside them during stressful tasks—silently.

5. Let them DJ the car ride without criticism.

6. Send them a meme that says 'I'm thinking of you.'

7. Remember their favorite snack— and surprise them with it.

Kavya, a mother from Hyderabad, once said, 'I kept trying to teach him. One day I stopped. I just started listening. And that's when he started talking.'

Sometimes, the strongest message you can send is this: I'm here. Not to fix. But to stay. And your child— your nearly-grown, silent, scrolling, sarcastic teen—will remember that long after the words are forgotten.

Because bonds aren't built in perfect moments. They're built in consistent ones.

Chapter 9: Parenting with Mindfulness

"The best way to capture moments is to pay attention. This is how we cultivate mindfulness." — Jon Kabat-Zinn

In the chaos of exams, phone pings, work calls, and school buses, parenting can feel like a marathon you didn't train for. And often, the first casualty of that rush is attention. Mindful parenting is the antidote—not to stress itself, but to how we meet it.

Mindfulness is not just meditation. It's being present. With curiosity, not control. With awareness, not assumption. When you look at your child, are you seeing them? Or are you seeing your own expectations projected onto them?

In Bengaluru, 15-year-old Aisha once said, "My dad asks how I'm doing while checking emails. So I don't answer anymore." Her father loved her deeply—but she didn't feel it. Because presence cannot be multitasked.

Parenting with mindfulness means listening to the silence behind the words. It means noticing the slouch in their shoulders, the delay in their laugh, the way they say 'fine' but mean 'please ask again.' It's being fully there, not just physically, but emotionally and energetically.

From the Bhagavad Gita to Buddhist teachings, Indian and Eastern philosophy is rich in reminders to observe without attachment. To act without ego. As Krishna says to Arjuna, 'Be steadfast in yoga, O Arjuna. Perform your duty and abandon all attachment to success or failure.' That's parenting too.

Try these practices to bring mindfulness into your parenting

without needing to change your
entire lifestyle:

*1. When your teen speaks, pause.
Don't interrupt. Let them finish even
if you disagree.*

*2. Before reacting, ask yourself: 'Am
I responding to their need—or my
fear?'*

*3. Start or end the day with 5
minutes of quiet presence together—
no agenda.*

*4. Replace 'Should' thoughts ('They
should know better') with 'Could'
questions ('What could be going on
for them?').*

*5. When angry, label your emotion
aloud: 'I'm feeling overwhelmed.' It
models emotional regulation.*

*6. Do one chore together mindfully—
folding clothes, washing dishes—
without phones.*

7. Reflect weekly: 'Did I see my child this week, or just manage them?'

Parenting isn't about perfection. It's about presence. When you practice mindful awareness, your child learns—not through lecture, but through your way of being.

Because in the end, your presence—calm, conscious, and compassionate—is the most powerful gift you can offer your growing teen.

Author's Note

This book was not written from a mountaintop. It was written from the ground—where real families live, where emotions run deep, and where parenting often feels like groping in the dark while hoping you're holding the right hand.

As a teacher, mentor, and parent, I've had the privilege of witnessing the extraordinary complexity of teenagers—their brilliance, their struggles, their contradictions. And just as often, I've seen the pain and confusion of parents who are trying—really trying—but don't always know how to bridge the widening gap.

If there's one thing I hope this book offers, it's reassurance: You don't need to be perfect. You don't need to have all the answers. You just need to show up—with presence, with patience, and with humility.

Your child isn't looking for a hero.
They're looking for a human.
Someone who listens. Someone who
stays. Someone who grows alongside
them.

I'm grateful to the many parents,
teens, counselors, and teachers who
shared their stories and wisdom.
Their courage and vulnerability
shaped every chapter.

May you return to these pages in
your toughest moments, not for
instruction—but for reminder. That
you're not alone. That you're doing
better than you think. And that love,
when offered consistently and
without condition, always leaves a
mark—even if you don't see it right
away.

Thank you for reading. Thank you
for parenting.

With warmth and hope,

— Venkata Krishna Rao Machineni

About the Author

Venkata Krishna Rao Machineni is an educator, mentor, and parenting guide with over two decades of experience in teaching and mentoring students preparing for competitive examinations like IIT-JEE and NEET. A postgraduate in Physics from IIT Madras, he is deeply passionate about shaping not only students' academic lives but also their emotional and psychological growth.

As an educator and the founder of VIJNA Academy, he has mentored thousands of teenagers and guided countless parents through the intricate journey of raising adolescents. His holistic approach—one that blends academic rigor with emotional intelligence—has earned him the trust and gratitude of families across India.

This book is an extension of his mission: to empower parents with the insight, patience, and presence needed to support their teens through life's most transformative years.